Resilience

A COLLECTION OF EMPOWERING SONGS OF WOMEN IN NEWFOUNDLAND AND LABRADOR

COMPILED AND ARRANGED BY
ROSEMARY LAWTON

CITADEL HOUSE PUBLISHING

DEDICATION

To all the strong women of this province

Published & Distributed by Citadel House Publishing
104 Main Street, Lewisporte,
NL, Canada, A0G 3B0

ISBN: 978-1-7753567-2-1

Cover Photo: "Ice Pans" by Tom Cochrane

Cover Photo: "Woman Carrying Water," 1952, Maritime History Archive, Memorial University. PF-317.744. Resettlement Photograph Collection

© 2019 by Rosemary Lawton

CONTENTS

INTRODUCTION 2
ACKNOWLEDGEMENTS 3
ABOUT THE SONGS 4

THE SONGS

1 A Cruel Wife 14
2 A Man In Love 16
3 The Banks of Sweet Dundee 18
4 Barney Flew Over the Hills to His Darling 20
5 Brave Ann O'Neil 22
6 Captain Wedderburn's Courtship 24
7 Caroline and Her Young Sailor Bold 26
8 Fair Marjorie's Ghost 28
9 The Golden Glove 30
10 Gold Watch 32
11 Gold Watch and Chain 34
12 The Irish Colleen 36
13 Lady Margaret 38
14 The Lovely Lowland Maid 40
15 Maiden Who Dwelt by the Shore 42
16 Old Woman 44
17 The Outlandish Knight 46
18 The Press Gang 48
19 The Pride of the Shamrock Shore 50
20 The Rose of Britain's Isle 52
21 Rosy Banks of Green 54
22 The Soldier Maid 56
23 Willy Taylor 58
REFERENCES AND RESOURCES 60
ABOUT THE AUTHOR 61

INTRODUCTION

While traveling across the province as a musician and listening to numerous traditional Newfoundland and Labrador musicians perform, I began to hear a repeating theme: "It is difficult to find an empowering ballad about women in Newfoundland and Labrador." Looking deeper into that statement, it became clear that this is, indeed, an issue. The history of the province: stories of sailors going off to sea, men fighting in wars, and everyday people dealing with the harsh realities of the rugged lands we live in are prominent fodder for songs that define who we are as Newfoundlanders and Labradorians. Resilience is a key descriptor in our identity, but where are the women? In the famous songs of this province, women often appear as love interests or damsels in distress, but the women of Newfoundland and Labrador are so much more than that.

I took the statement "it is difficult to find an empowering ballad about women in Newfoundland and Labrador" as a challenge. I spoke to numerous traditional musicians about this concept and in my efforts to find ballads to fit this theme, I was pointed in the direction of some prominent field researchers who did various recordings and transcriptions of ballads and songs in the province. These researchers are: Elizabeth B. Greenleaf, Grace Y. Mansfield, Maud Karpeles, MacEdward Leach, and Kenneth Peacock. With their research supporting my ideas, I was able to compile twenty-three traditional songs that tell stories of empowering women in Newfoundland and Labrador. These stories paint women as intelligent, resourceful, and strong. There are tales of heroines, villains, and everything in between. What amazed me most was that many of these songs were written centuries ago, which means the concept of empowered women in the province has existed for a very long time.

ACKNOWLEDGEMENTS

Special thanks to Anita Best, Pamela Morgan, Eleanor Dawson, Ellen Power, Jean Hewson, Colleen Field, Linda Byrne, Linda White, Emily Felix, Sarah Antle, Jasmine Stairs, Nicholas Earle, Jim Payne, Hugh Scott, The Folklore Department at Memorial University of Newfoundland, the Stairs family and my own family for helping to make this project what it is today.

A special thanks to the archives that housed the photos for this book including: The Rooms Provincial Archives, The Dr. Henry N. Payne Community Museum, Archives and Special Collections at Memorial University of Newfoundland, The Maritime History Archive, The Trinity Historical Society and the Nurse Myra Bennett Foundation.

This project is funded in part by FACTOR, the Government of Canada and Canada's private radio broadcasters. Ce projet est financé en partie par FACTOR, le gouvernement du Canada et les radiodiffuseurs privés du Canada.

ABOUT THE SONGS

GREENLEAF AND MANSFIELD: BALLADS AND SEA SONGS OF NEWFOUNDLAND

GOLD WATCH – Sung by Mr. Will White, Sandy Cove, 1929 (Greenleaf and Mansfield, 110-111).
It takes a while for the listener to realize what this song is truly about and I believe that this is because it is from the male perspective. From the man's perspective of the story, he meets a beautiful maiden who is far too virtuous to let him have his way with her. Eventually he convinces her to stay the night with him, but only if he pays her (this should have been an indicator of what was to come…). After their night together, the man awakes to find that his gold watch has been stolen and the girl is nowhere in sight. By the end of the song, it is revealed that she was no maiden. She was a madam.

MAIDEN WHO DWELT BY THE SHORE – Sung by Mrs. Annie Walters, Rocky Harbour, 1929 (Greenleaf and Mansfield, 63-64).
This song was made famous first by Pamela Morgan, and then by prominent Newfoundland band "the Once," and has been recorded many times over the years, maintaining its status as a truly bold and empowering song.

Who doesn't love a tale of an epic escape? This maiden was happily living alone on the shore when a captain decided that she was the object of his desire and bribed his crew to get her on board his ship. After capturing her, she is placed in the captain's cabin below decks where she sings the captain and sailors to sleep, robs them of all their riches, and uses a sword to paddle her way back to shore. Not only has she outwitted her captors to earn her own freedom, she returned home as a much wealthier woman. That will teach people not to mess with this maiden!

KARPELES: FOLK SONGS FROM NEWFOUNDLAND

A MAN IN LOVE - Sung by Mrs. Susan Dusey, Marystown, Placentia Bay, 1930 (Karpeles, 194-195).
Is it the story of a woman who waited too long, or a woman who ran out of patience? This seems to be the debate of "A Man in Love." I think it depends on who you think the speaker is. My interpretation of the story goes as such: A man and a woman have been courting for 7 years, despite the disapproval of the gentleman's parents. Always promising that someday the couple will be married, he returns from sea and asks to stay the night in the lady's room. This is a scandalous request for the time period, especially out of wedlock because it could easily paint the woman as a person of ill repute. She denies the gentleman's request, proclaims that she is tired of waiting for him, and sends him off to sea. In the last verse, the gentleman bids farewell and claims that he will never return.

I believe that the woman in this song is claiming her independence. She is tired of waiting, and refuses that her name be sullied by letting the gentleman stay the night. I see his request to stay the night as the proverbial "straw that broke the camel's back" leading to the end of their relationship.

THE OUTLANDISH KNIGHT – Sung by Mr. Matthew Aylward, Stock Cove, Bonavista Bay, 1929 (Karpeles, 23-24).
This is the first song that I found with the theme of empowering women at the forefront. This song fully encompasses the theme of the project by telling the tale of a kidnapped woman in her fight for survival. A fairy knight takes the woman in this story from her home, and threatens to drown her. He sees that her robe could be expensive and demands for her to take it off before he drowns her so he can sell it. The lady feigns modesty by asking her captor to turn his back to her while she disrobes, and while his back is turned, she pushes him in the water instead. The woman in this story is resourceful, intelligent, and strong. She is a true role model for women of the past and present.

THE PRESS GANG - Sung by Mr. William Malloy, St. Shotts, St. Mary's Bay, 1930 (Karpeles, 176-168).
A theme that I discovered throughout some of these songs was women who dress up as men to go off to sea or fight in wars. I learned that these songs actually fit into a genre called "Jacket and Trouser Songs" because enough of this kind of song exists to establish a genre of their own.

What intrigued me in "The Press Gang" was the fact that while Ellen (the lady in the story) was in disguise on the ship, she claimed to be an astrologer. Throughout history astrologers were considered to be scholars. It is very powerful that Ellen acknowledges her intelligence to her true love because (even though she is in disguise), once she reveals herself, he can now see her in her truest form. This is a great song following the theme of female identity.

THE ROSE OF BRITAIN'S ISLE - Sung by Mrs. Lizzie Mahoney, Stock Cove, Bonavista Bay, 1929 (Karpeles, 173-174).
This is another "Jacket and Trousers Song." In this song, the Lady Jane becomes a heroine after dressing as a man and going to sea to find her true love, who has been sent away by her disapproving father. While at sea, an enemy ship attacks their vessel and Jane takes a bullet in order to save her dear Edwin. They return home to find that Jane's father has passed away, leaving Jane with the family fortune. She is now free to marry Edwin without the weight of her father's disapproval.

In many of the songs I looked at for this book, I came across countless stories resembling a Shakespearian tragedy featuring disapproving fathers who send their daughters' true loves away. Often in these songs, the daughter stabs herself in the chest or falls into a depression and withers away until her life is snuffed out. This leaves a mourning father to regret ever separating the two lovers. "The Rose of Britain's Isle" is a refreshing take on this kind of song because Jane takes matters into her own hands and fights her way back to her true love. This is not a tale of defeat, but of strength, and resilience.

LEACH: FOLK BALLADS AND SONGS OF THE LOWER LABRADOR COAST

A CRUEL WIFE - Sung by Mr. Stuart Letto, Lance au Clair, 1960 (Leach282-283).
Comedy is the flavour of the day in this foolish tale. "A Cruel Wife" bears a strong resemblance to the well-known song, "The Old Woman From Wexford." With some melodic differences, the story remains the same: an old woman is tired of being married to her husband and is searching for an escape so she can be with another man. A doctor provides her with a way to make her husband blind so she can drown him in the river. The old man figures out what she is trying to do and fights back. The song ends at an impasse while the old couple battles it out in the river.

I chose to include this song for three reasons: I liked that this was a different take on a classic song and that it got passed down, surviving in Labrador. I also enjoyed the fact that the elderly couple were an equal match for each other. Nobody wins and I find that refreshing. Lastly, I wanted to highlight the fact that there are a number of songs like this one. If you line these songs up with societal issues of the time, divorce was not only frowned upon, it was social suicide. For people locked in a bad marriage, the only idea of escape was social ruin or to be widowed. I think this type of song brings to light a much bigger issue of the time, and to some extent, of our time too.

THE BANKS OF SWEET DUNDEE - Sung by Mr. Peter Letto, Lance au Clair, 1960 (Leach, 60-61).

This song starts off resembling a Cinderella story, but there is no fairy godmother in this tale. Mary has to take matters into her own hands; she has a rich father who tragically passes away, leaving her with her evil uncle, who has control over her money and estate. He attempts to marry her off to a Squire who ends up attacking Mary in her uncle's field. In her efforts to escape, she steals the Squire's pistol and kills him. In her uncle's rage after discovering this, he attempts to kill Mary and she uses the pistol to kill her uncle too. She sends for a doctor and a lawyer who wills her uncle's gold to Mary and she lives happily ever after as a very rich woman.

BARNEY FLEW OVER THE HILLS TO HIS DARLING - Sung by Mr. Ned Odell, Pinware, 1960 (Leach, 88-89).

This song falls under the category of a "Night Visit Song" (A song that tells the story of a person who receives a late-night visitor). It talks of a gentlemen caller named Barney who requests entry to the estate of a young woman named Katy late at night with one obvious intention: to spend the night in Katy's bed. There is a back and forth conversation where Barney is trying to convince Katy to let him in but she is unmoving and sends him home instead. What is refreshing about this song is that Barney does not "win" the heart of the lady in his efforts to convince her. She stands her ground and refuses to be persuaded to do something she has no desire in doing. This is something that is often neglected in love stories. The pursuit of a man is considered desirable, however sometimes a woman is just not interested.

BRAVE ANN O'NEIL (ALSO KNOWN AS SWEET ANN O'NEIL) - Sung by Mr. Ned Odell, Pinware, 1960 (Leach, 90-91).

If you are looking for a story where the woman comes out as the hero, this is the song for you. "Brave Ann O'Neil" tells the story of a man named Chris who has been wrongly accused of a crime and is walking to the gallows to be hung. Each step he takes towards his death is a verse in the song, and at each verse, he comes across someone he loves. The first step he takes, he sees his sister, whom he gives a ring to remember him by. The second step he takes, he sees his brother and asks him where his true love is. Finally, on his last step, he sees his true love, Ann O'Neil, riding in on a horse with papers that are signed by the king that prove Chris' innocence. She would not accept her true love's fate and refused to stand by him and watch him be wrongfully taken. Because of her bravery and determination she was able to save Chris' life and become the hero of his story.

CAPTAIN WEDDERBURN'S COURTSHIP - Sung by Mr. Martin Hocko, Pinware, 1960 (Leach, 26-29).

This is a clever song that portrays an encounter between the Virgin Mary and the Devil. The Devil is holding Mary hostage and she must outwit him by answering six riddles. If she fails to answer them, she will have to "lie with [him] beneath the old stone wall." The devil chooses his questions with the assumption that he will win this game, and Mary will be forced to lie with him. However Mary surprises him by answering each riddle with ease. She then banishes the Devil, and he has no choice but to leave. It is apparent throughout the song that Mary is the one who holds the power in this encounter. The Devil doesn't stand a chance.

The lyrics of this song are accompanied by a beautiful melody, giving it even more depth and strength.

OLD WOMAN - Sung by Mr. Henry Belben, Lance au Loup, 1960 (Leach, 292-293).

This song tells the tale of an old trickster who is searching for a way to prank her sweetheart. She places a pile of crockery ware (plates and dishes) on a chair behind her bedroom door and turns off all the lights. When her sweetheart comes to find her in the night, he creates utter chaos. He tips the chair over and the crockery ware is sent crashing to the ground. She proceeds to make him pay for all the damages while feigning innocence and the gentleman ends the song by warning his friends to never go courting in the dark.

THE ROSY BANKS OF GREEN - Sung by Mr. Ned Odell, Pinware, 1960 (Leach, 326).

This song features a disapproving father who seriously regrets getting his way, when his decisions end in the death of his own daughter. The parent featured in this type of song is called a "Ballad Parent." In this case, the father is the "Ballad Parent" and disapproves of a relationship between his daughter Josephine and a young sailor. He decides to prevent his daughter's union with the sailor by shooting him. His daughter is too quick however and jumps in front of the bullet. The bullet did as bullets do, and maintained a straight and true course hitting both lovers. As the couple lies dying, Josephine uses her last breath to make her father rue the day he chose to change her fate.

I chose to include this song because of Josephine's bravery in trying to save her sailor from her father. I appreciate her efforts to make her father regret his decisions and look back on this day as the day he selfishly tried to take control of her life. The melody of this song is very haunting in a natural minor key, which drew me to pursue it further.

WILLY TAYLOR - Sung by Mr. Stuart Letto, Lance au Clair, 1960 (Leach, 314-315).
Sorry gentlemen, we are not on your side with this one! This is a "Jacket and Trousers Song" that talks of a couple who were seconds away from getting married in a church with their friends and family, when a crowd of sailors come into the church to press young Willy off to sea. His bride to be is not happy about this, so it doesn't take long before she follows suit, dressed as a man named Richard Carr. After searching the sea for seven long years, she finds herself on the ship whose captain was responsible for taking her Willy away from her. She confronts the captain who points her in the direction of the docks where she sees Willy, walking with his new bride. The lady calmly calls for the sailors to bring her two pistols, which she uses to shoot and kill Willy. The captain of the ship hears of this and makes her first lieutenant on board his ship, leaving her to sail the ocean wide for the rest of her life with a sword in each hand.

PEACOCK – SONGS OF THE NEWFOUNDLAND OUTPORTS

CAROLINE AND HER YOUNG SAILOR BOLD - Sung by Mr. Chris Cobb, Barred Island, 1952 (Peacock, 329-330).
One more "Jacket and Trousers Song" for you. Told to stay home with her parents, Caroline did the complete opposite by dressing as a gallant young sailor to sail the ocean wide with her love William. They sailed for three years and were shipwrecked three times. After all adventures were said and done, they returned home and requested permission from Caroline's father to be married. Her father, who never had any issues with the couple to begin with, consents for them to be wed and shortly after, they marry and live happily ever after on the fortune that Caroline has earned while at sea.

In this song, Caroline truly goes against any expectations of gender for the time and does what she wants, rather than seeking the favour of her community. Not only does she dress up as a man to go off to sea, but she also survives three shipwrecks to return home with her own fortune. For this time period, it was very uncommon and taboo for the woman to have her own fortune. She is completely self-sufficient and can share her success with someone she loves. It is also uncommon for the gentleman of this era to support the kind of relationship dynamic where the woman provides for the man financially, so this is a very forward-thinking song.

FAIR MARJORIE'S GHOST - Sung by Mrs. Clara Stevens, Bellburns, 1959 (Peacock, 383-384).
After her death, Fair Marjorie discovers that her true love has moved on and married someone else. Hearing this news, she jumps out her window and appears in Willy's room where she confronts him as a ghost. She asks him how he likes his bed, his sheets, and his new bride who lies asleep in his arms. In his fear of seeing the ghost of his lost love, he tries to appease Fair Marjorie by telling her what he thinks she wants to hear. He tells her that he loves his bed and his sheets, but he would prefer to have Fair Marjorie instead of his new bride. Fair Marjorie is enraged by this false statement and smites Willy, who falls at her feet, never to kiss a woman again.

GOLD WATCH AND CHAIN - Sung by Mr. Freeman Bennett, St. Paul's, 1958 (Peacock, 342-343).

In traditional Newfoundland and Labrador music there is a kind of tune called a "crooked tune." Many tunes written in this province have a crooked lilt to them. The descriptor, "crooked" is used to indicate that in each bar, beats can be added or taken away, which would jolt the listener and keep them engaged. This is very prominent in instrumental music, however; it can also be found in traditional songs as well. This particular song was originally rhythmically "crooked" to a point where it was impossible to sing. I tried rewriting it in numerous time signatures and eventually decided upon 4/4, which I was able to stay true to, with the exception of a handful of measures in 2/4. The melody is so interesting that I did not want to completely rewrite the tune because I did not want to lose the integrity of the music.

The song itself is another "Jacket and Trousers Song" that tells the story of a girl who decides to dress up as a sailor and rob her true love. In the process of robbing him however, her true love refuses to give up a diamond ring. He proclaims that it is a "pledge of love" and is willing to lose his life before losing the ring. She realizes how true his love really is and flees the scene of the crime. The next day as they are out walking together, the gentleman sees the maiden wearing his gold watch and chain. She admits that it was she who robbed him the day before, and returns his watch and chain to him. Shocked at hearing this, her true love admits that if he'd had his pistols, he would have shot her and then, after discovering her true identity, he would have mourned for the love he'd slain.

THE GOLDEN GLOVE - Sung by Mr. Everett Bennett, St. Paul's, 1958 (Peacock, 340-341).
This is a very cute "Jacket and Trousers" song where the lady ends up cleverly manipulating her way into love. The lady of this tale is a rich merchant, which is a rare and special occupation for a woman to have during this time. She is set to marry a squire, but during his bachelor party, she sees that one of his groomsmen is a very handsome farmer and decides that she wants to marry him instead. She doesn't say another word to the squire before leaving to pursue the farmer and sets out to think of a plan to win her new man. She dresses up in a waistcoat and britches (which can be used as another name for a "Jacket and Trousers Song"), takes her dog and her gun, and goes out hunting near the farmer's field. When the farmer enters the field, she approaches him in her disguise and claims to have found a golden glove, which secretly belongs to her. She gives the farmer the glove she has "found" and goes home where she puts up a public notice announcing that she will marry whoever finds her lost glove. The farmer very honourably approaches the lady with her glove and the two are married shortly after. It is not until after they are married that the lady tells the farmer the trickery she performed in order to win him, where he is now safely ensnared in her love.

I love this song because the lady in the story firmly goes against any societal expectations of gender at the time. She is in a position of power from the very beginning as a merchant, which was a very sought after position for men. She proceeds to boldly and strongly move on her romantic feelings, refusing to feel trapped in any relationship. She then dresses up as a man, but uses her own dog and gun to hunt near the farmer's field. She is intelligent, strong, and completely in control, which I truly admire.

THE IRISH COLLEEN - Sung by Mr. Patrick W. Nash, Branch, 1961 (Peacock, 366-367).
"The Irish Colleen" is a drinking song. I find this song very amusing because it is such a friendly conversation between a group of women who are loyal to their countries. There is a girl from Ireland, Scotland, Wales, and England. They have an intense debate on whose country is best. Each woman is unwavering in their own loyal opinions but the song remains a celebration. The song is sung from the perspective of a proud Irish woman so each chorus is a cheers to old Ireland.

So often, women are pitted against each other in stories. It is a nice change to see a story where there could be a hostile debate, but instead the result is support and pride.

LADY MARGARET - Sung by Mr. Mike Kent, Cape Broyle, 1951 (Peacock, 390-391).
I had a lot of difficulty deciding whether or not I should include a love song in this project. After a lot of thought however, I realized that love in its purest form is extremely empowering. There is a saying that a couple is stronger together than they are apart. I first heard a recording of Emile Benoit singing this song, and the haunting lyrics drew me in. I've seen it written in English and French, but when I came across this song in the Peacock edition, it had a different melody than I had ever heard, so I knew it had to be included.

A gentleman has passed away, but before he leaves this earth, he goes to visit his dear Lady Margaret one last time. The two go for a walk together, laughing and sharing stories, and when the night is nearing its end, Lady Margaret asks if there is room in his grave for her to join him. He explains that his parents are by his head and feet, and he is surrounded by three hellhounds because he has sinned and they are preventing him from moving on to the next life. One hellhound is for drinking too much, another is for being too proud, and the last one is for promising his true love that one day they will be married; a promise that he will never be able to fulfill. Lady Margaret then takes out a cross and blesses him, cleansing him of his sins. By this act, Lady Margaret makes it possible for her love to move on, so they bid one last farewell and her love dissolves into the night. Lady Margaret knows in her heart that one day they will be together again, which brings her peace.

THE LOVELY LOWLAND MAID - Sung by Mr. Patrick Rossiter, Fermeuse, 1961.
Not every empowering song can have the women be the hero. Sometimes we need a villain too, and oh boy, do we ever get one in this song. Mary Ann is originally portrayed as a "Lovely Lowland Maid" who is being pursued by a supposedly poor sailor. The sailor approaches his true love multiple times but is turned down because he is poor. Once he reveals his hidden riches however, his love changes her mind, thus showing her true colours. At this point, the story strongly resembles the song "Jack the Sailor," where at this point in the story, the sailor sees the greed in his supposed true love, and leaves her behind to regret ever doubting him. In "The Lovely Lowland Maid" however, the song takes a darker approach. After the sailor realizes his love is only interested in his money, he leaves her and goes to sleep in the barn. Mary Ann goes to another of her lovers and convinces him to rob the sailor. When they go to the barn at night, Mary Ann pulls out a dagger, and not only do they rob him, they murder him too. The writer does not let Mary Ann get away with this vengeful act though. The grounds keeper was secretly watching and reports the two murderers, where they are arrested and condemned to die for their crimes. Not all stories can have a happy ending, can they?

THE PRIDE OF THE SHAMROCK SHORE - Sung by Mr. Peter Ryan, Aquaforte, 1961.

This is a harrowing tale of mistaken identity and loss. A man named Henry is sent off to war and leaves his true love behind. After years of being apart, Henry returns home to see that his true love Mary has moved on with a squire and does not recognize him. He then decides that if Mary forsakes her squire and pledges herself to him, that he will forgive her. Mary laughs at this and sends Henry away (Which to be fair, if you did not know this man who is demanding that you pledge yourself to him, you would probably do the same thing). He refuses to leave, which leads the squire to threaten him, triggering a battle. Henry shoots and kills the squire, and then Mary takes her fallen lover's weapon and uses it to kill Henry. It is not until she sees a fallen token on the ground belonging to her lost love, that she realizes Henry was indeed who he claimed to be, but now it is too late. Both lovers are gone. In horror after this realization, she flees the scene of the crime. Not long after she is picked up, charged with murder, and left in a dungeon to live out the rest of her days.

To the people who ask the question "how could she have forgotten what her true love looks like?" it is actually plausible that this could have happened. To put this into context, back in the day that this story takes place, technology was limited, making correspondence difficult. People kept in touch by writing letters, and if a young man left for war and returned home years later after losing correspondence, he would have physically changed a great deal. When a stranger approaches you and tells you to pledge your love to them, what would you do? Fall into their arms willingly? I praise Mary for standing her ground and trying to protect her lover and herself.

THE SOLDIER MAID - Sung by Mrs. Clara Stevens, Bellburns, 1959 (Peacock, 346-347).

Another "Jacket and Trousers Song," "The Soldier Maid" tells a slightly different story than the others. This is not a song about love, but a song about pride. Orphaned as a child, a young girl was mistaken as a boy and taken in by the army, where she was taught to be the best drummer the world had ever seen. She fought in many battles, but she was so valuable as a drummer that her general feared that she would be killed in battle. In his efforts to protect his best drummer, the general sent her to London to take charge of the tower. While in London, she met a young lady who fell in love with her however, upon discovering her secret identity, she was betrayed to the army. The general laughed at the fact that he never figured out his error but is forced to discharge the soldier maid. She proclaims proudly at the end of the song that if the army is ever in need, she will "boldly stand with sword in hand to fight for [England] again."

NOTE:

I chose to organize these songs by song collector because, while I have compiled the songs of this subject matter in one place, I fully credit Greenleaf, Mansfield, Karpeles, Leach, and Peacock for the work that they did. If it were not for these collectors, many of these songs would have faded away. With this collection of songs, I hope to rekindle a love for these stories so they can live on for future generations.

1
A Cruel Wife
(Dover)

Traditional
Arr. Rosemary Lawton

There was an old wo-man from Do - ver, in Do - ver she did dwell; She dear - ly loved her hus - band but a - no - ther one twice as well. with me rad - dle dum, da - dle dum, da - dle dum, with me rad - dle dum, da - dle dum dee. With me ra - dle dum da - dle dum da - dle-dum Right fo - le - ro rid-dle o dee. She

2. She went unto the doctor
   To see what she could find,
   Saying, "Dr. McGhee, tell me,
   What will make my poor man blind?"

Reprise:
With me raddle-dum, daddle-dum, daddle-dum,
With me raddle-dum, daddle-dum, dee.
With me raddle-dum, daddle-dum, daddle-dum,
Right folero riddle o dee.

3. You go and get some marrow bone;
   You grind it fine and small
   Before it gets it half drunk,
   He won't see you at all."

4. She went and got the marrow bone;
   She grind it fine and small;
   Before he got it half drunk,
   He couldn't see her at all.

5. "Now I'm blind and feeble
   This world I cannot stay;
   I will go and drown myself,
   If you show me the way."

6. She led him to the river side,
   She led him to the brim;
   "Indeed I will not drown myself,
   If you won't push me in."

7. She put her hand before her eyes,
   Just to shove him in;
   The little old man, he jumped one side,
   The old woman she went in.

8. She went unto the bottom,
   And she began to bawl.
   "O my, my lovely Nancy,
   I can't see you at all."

9. She went unto the bottom;
   She came up to the brim;
   The little old man with his walking stick,
   He popped her in again.

10. "Oh, don't you see me coming,
    Oh, can't you read me mind,
    Oh, don't you see me coming
    With the peak of me cap behind."

2
A Man In Love

Traditional
Arr. Rosemary Lawton

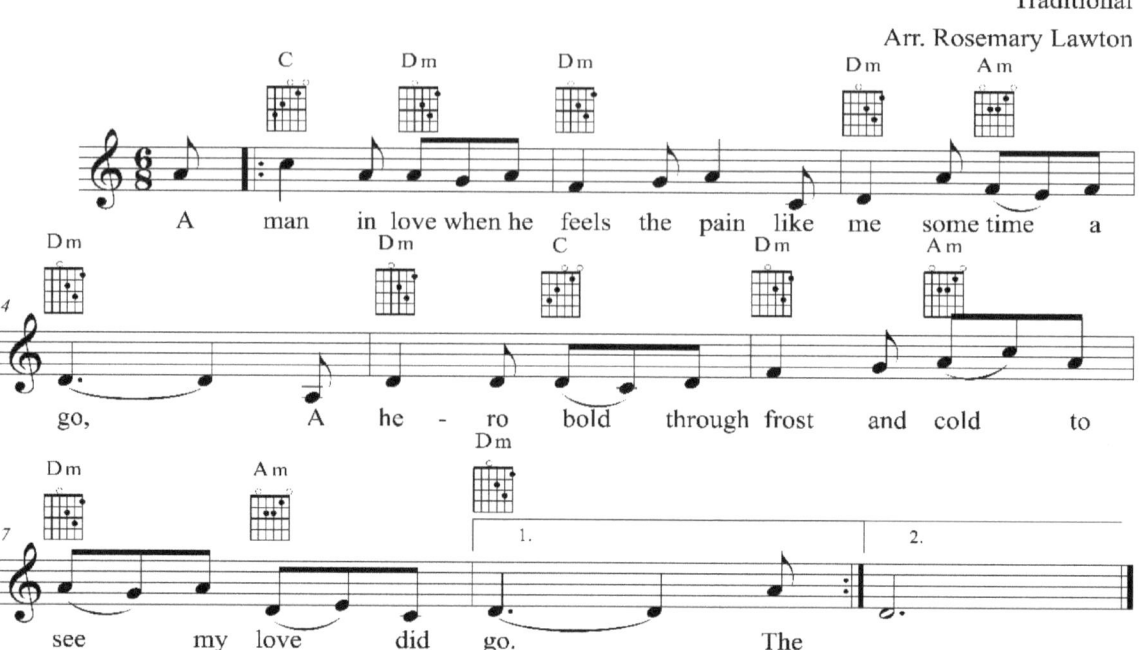

2. The moon shone bright to show me light
   Along my dreary way,
   And when I came to my own love's house
   I knocked at the door so low.

3. She got up and she let me in,
   Most lively I did go.
   With her step so light and her voice so sweet,
   Her hair in ringlets flowed.

4. I stole one kiss from her ruby lips
   Where all my fancy goes.
   I stole one kiss from her ruby lips
   Where all my fancy goes.

5. Will you go to your room, I said.
   Or will you go to your bed,
   Or will you go to some lonely grove?
   The morning we'll be wed.

6. I will not go to my room, she said,
   Young man, you'll never prove true.
   I'll sit you down by the fireside,
   In the morning I'll see you.

7. Seven long years I courted you
   Against your parents will,
   Always intending to marry you,
   But now my love, farewell.

8. My ship lies off in the harbour,
   She's bound to Columby's shore,
   So I bid adieu to my true love,
   Here's adieu for evermore.

"Industrial": Jessie Luther supervises the construction of a kiln with Mr. Holley, St. Anthony, Sept. 1908, The Rooms Provincial Archives, VA 118-93.4, International photograph collection.

3
The Banks of Sweet Dundee
(Undaunted Mary)

Traditional
Arr. Rosemary Lawton

It's of a merchant's daughter, most beautiful I'm told.
Her father died and left her with five thousand pounds in gold.
She lived with her uncle, the cause of all her woe;
You soon may hear how this affair it proved his overthrow. Her

2. Her uncle had a plowboy who Mary loved too well;
   Down her uncle's garden the talks of love do tell
   There was a wealthy squire who oftimes came her to see,
   But still she loved the plowboy on the Banks of Sweet Dundee.

3. Her uncle rose one morning and went to her straightaway,
   Tapping at her bedroom door, these words to her did say:
   "Arise, arise, you fair one, a lady you shall be,
   The squire's waiting for you on the Banks of Sweet Dundee."

4. "A fig for all your squires, your lords, and dukes likewise,
   For Willie he appears to me like diamonds in my eyes."
   "Begone, begone, you cruel one, a lady you'll not be,
   For I mean to banish Willie from the Banks of Sweet Dundee."

5. The press gang came for Willie when he was all alone;
   He dearly fought for liberty but there was six to one."
   The blood did flow in torrents. "Pray kill me now," said he,
   "For I mean to fight for Mary on the Banks of Sweet Dundee."

6. As Mary was a walking, lamenting for her love,
   She met this wealthy squire down in her uncle's grove.
   He threw his arms around her "Begone young man." Said she,
   "For you've banished my true love from the Banks of Sweet Dundee."

7. He clasped his arms around her, thinking to throw her down,
   Two pistols and a sword she saw beneath his morning gown.
   The pistols she took from him; the sword he used full free.
   Mary fired and shot the squire, on the Banks of Sweet Dundee.

8. Her uncle overheard the noise and hastened to the ground
   "Since you have shot the squire, I'll give you your death wound."
   "Stand off, stand off," said Mary, "For daunted I'll not be."
   The trigger drew and her uncle slew on the Banks of Sweet Dundee.

9. The doctor then was sent for, a man of noble skill.
   And likewise a lawyer for to write and sign his will.
   He willed his gold to Mary, who fought so wilfully,
   And he closed his eyes, no more to rise on the Banks of Sweet Dundee.

4
Barney Flew Over the Hills to His Darling
(Barney and Katie)

Traditional
Arr. Rosemary Lawton

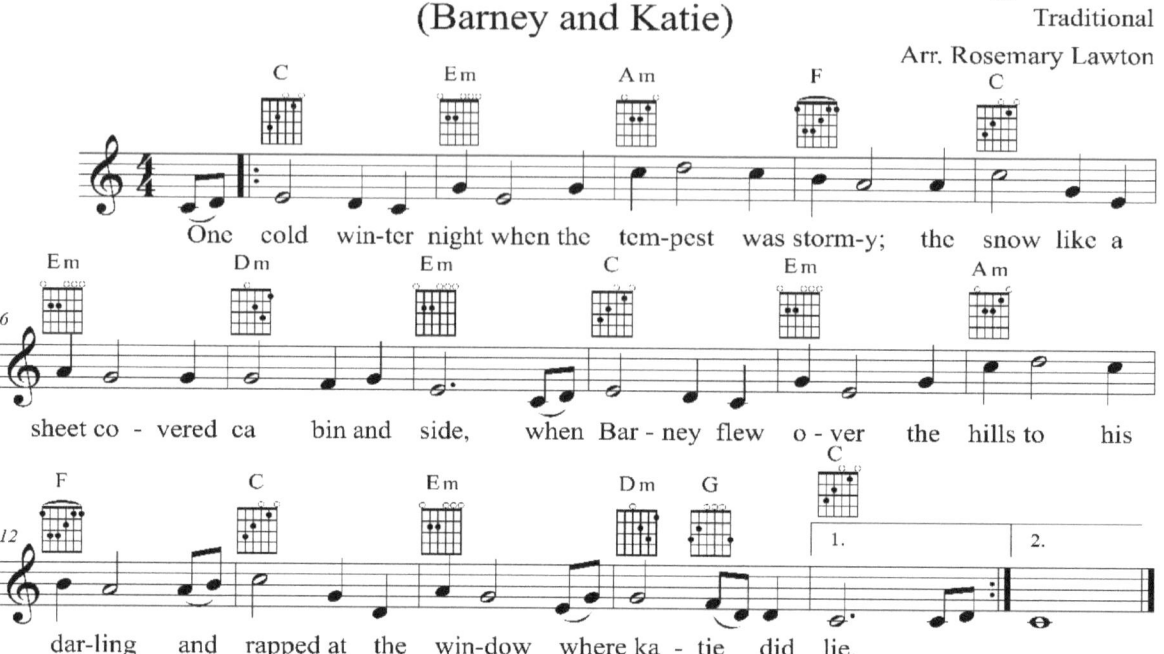

One cold winter night when the tempest was stormy; the snow like a sheet covered cabin and side, when Barney flew over the hills to his darling and rapped at the window where katie did lie.

2. "Adieu all," said he. "Are you asleep or awaking;
   It's a bitter cold night and my coat it is thin;
   The storm it is brewing, the frost it's a making,
   And Kathleen Mavarney won't you let me in?"

3. "Barney," said dear Katie as she spoke through the window,
   "How can you be taking us out of our bed
   To come at this time it would be a shame to
   The wind it has gotten into your head.

4. "If your heart it was true of my fame you'd be tender,
   Consider the time when there's nobody in,
   What have a poor girl but her name to defend her,
   No Barney, my Barney, I won't let you in."

5. "I believe," said he, "sure your eyes is a fountain,
   'Twould weep for the love I might lie at your door,
   And your name is so white as the snow on the mountain,
   And Barney will die to preserve it as pure."

6. "I will go to my home where the winter can't face me,
   I'll whistle and sing and I'll not be within
   And the words of my Katie will comfort and cheer me,
   No Barney, my Barney, I won't let you in."

"Frances Cluett in VAD Uniform," 1914-1918, 5.01.001, Archives and Special Collections, Memorial University of Newfoundland.

5
Brave Ann O'Neil

Traditional
Arr. Rosemary Lawton

My love he is one of the finest young men ever nature formed and the sun to shine on, And tomorrow morning the noble proscecutor sentenced Chris on the gallows to be hung. As

2. And as he rode through the streets of Derry,
   He rode so bold and undaunted seemed
   And he looked more like a man whose heart was broken
   Than any young man was condemned to die.

3. "Oh, hang him up," said the bloody sherrif,
   The sherrif and clerk were standing by,
   "Hold on, hold on, you bold prosecutor,
   I'll let you know he's not fit to die."

4. "You must hold on for half an hour
   Until confession with me is done
   And after that, you bold prosecutor,
   He can go off to the setting sun."

5. As he went up the first step on the gallows,
   His beloved sister he chanced to see;
   "Step up, step up, my beloved sister,
   I have a word to exchange with thee."

6. And taking a gold ring from off his finger,
   He wrapped it up in silk so fine,
   "Take this, take this, my beloved sister,
   And keep your dear brother close in your mind."

7. As he went up the next step on the gallows,
   His beloved brother he chanced to see,
   "step up, step up, my beloved brother;
   I have a word to exchange with thee."

8. "Where is my jewel, oh where is my darling
   She don't come here for to visit me.
   Do she think it's a shame or a scandal
   That I must die on the gallows tree?"

9. As he went up the last step on the gallows,
   His beloved sweetheart he chanced to see,
   As she came riding on her weary gelding,
   She rode so fast, as fast as could be.

10. "Come down, come down, from that weary gallows.
    I have your freedom from George, our king.
    In spite of all those bold prosecutors,
    I'll have you crowned in the blooming spring."

11. Now lads and lasses, fill up your glasses,
    Fill them up and never fail;
    You lads and lasses toss up your glasses,
    And drink a health to brave Ann O'Neill.

6
Captain Wedderburn's Courtship
(The Devil and the Blessed Virgin Mary)

Traditional
Arr. Rosemary Lawton

A girl roved out one evening to view her father's land. She met with a deep sea captain, he took her by the hand. He said unto his comraids, if it was not against the law, I'd have this fair one with me to lie beneath the cold stone wall. Hands

2. "Hands off, young man, hands off, young man, hands off, young man," said she.
   "I'm to view my father's dwelling, where the green grass grows so tall,
   So I won't comply with you to lie beneath the old stone wall.
   So I won't comply with you to lie beneath the old stone wall."

3. "I will put to you six questions and you'll fulfill them all:
   'What is deeper than the sea, what's higher than the wall?
   What's a young man's sense in a fair maid's heart, I you on duty call?
   And you'll comply with me to lie beneath the old stone wall."

4. "Now hell is deeper than the sea; the sun is higher than the wall.
   The Devil's sense in a fair maid's heart on you on duty call.
   I won't comply with you to lie beneath the old stone wall.
   I won't comply with you to lie beneath the old stone wall."

5. "Now what is deeper than the sea; what's higher than the wall?
   What bird sings best when the lark is at rest in the spring when the dew first fall,
   Nor you'll comply with me to lie beneath the old stone wall
   Nor you'll comply with me to lie beneath the old stone wall."

6. "Now hell is deeper than the sea; the sun is higher than the wall;
   The thrush sings best when the lark is at rest, in the spring when the dew first fall.
   I won't comply with you to lie beneath the old stone wall.
   I won't comply with you to lie beneath the old stone wall."

7. "For breakfast you must get for me a fish without a bone,
   And for dinner you must get me a cherry without a stone,
   And for my supper you must get me a bird without a gall
   Nor you'll comply with me to lie beneath the old stone wall."

8. "Now when the fish is first born, I'm sure it has no bone,
   And when the cherry is in full bloom, I'm certain it has no stone.
   The dove she is a gentle bird; she flies without a gall,
   So I won't comply with you to lie beneath the old stone wall."

9. "You must get for me some of the fruit that in September grew;
   You must get for me a silkworm cloak that a shuttle never went to;
   You must get me a sparrow's horn or yet on duty call
   Nor you'll comply with me to lie beneath the old stone wall."

10. "My father keeps some of the fruit that in September grew;
    My mother has a silk worm cloak that a shuttle never went through;
    A sparrow's horn is not hard to find; he has one on every claw.
    So I won't comply with you to lie beneath the old stone wall."

11. "There's a man outside my father's gate; he is waiting to come in;
    I am sure that man was never born, nor yet committed any sin;
    His mother's side was cruelly pierced if you on duty call.
    You fly from me, Devil," said she, "right through that old stone wall."

7
Caroline and Her Young Sailor Bold

Traditional
Arr. Rosemary Lawton

It's of a rich noblemen's daughter, Caroline was her name I'm told, and out of her drawing-room window she admired a young sailor bold. Her

2. Her teeth were so white as the ivory,
   Her hair so black as the jet;
   Caroline took her departure,
   And William she very soon met.

3. "Young maid, stay at home with your parents,
   And do from them as you are told,
   And never let anyone persuade you
   To follow a young sailor bold."

4. "I'll never let anyone persuade me,
   One moment and then I'll decide,
   I'll ship and go sailing with my true love
   Across the ocean so wide."

5. She shipped as a gallant young sailor
   Her jacket and trousers so blue,
   Three years and a half plowed the ocean,
   Caroline and her young sailor true.

6. Three times out of that she got shipwrecked,
   But she always proved loyal and true,
   A mizzen to a royal so lofty,
   Her jacket and trousers to blue.

7. Her father went weeping and wailing
   And the tears down his cheeks did roll
   Until the ship returned to old England
   Caroline and her young sailor bold.

8. "Oh father, dear father, forgive me,
   Do not persuade me with gold,
   There's only one question I'll ask you,
   Be true to my young sailor bold."

9. Her father admired young William
   And placed him in large unity,
   If life it is spared until morning,
   It's married this couple shall be.

10. They got married on Caroline's fortune,
    With twenty-five thousand in gold,
    And now they are living in splendour,
    Caroline and her young sailor bold.

"Girl carrying hoop and water buckets,"
Venison Tickle, Labrador (1920s)
The Rooms Provincial Archives, VA 104-33.2,
International Grenfell Association photograph
collection.

8
Fair Marjorie's Ghost
(Fair Margaret and Sweet William)

Traditional
Arr. Rosemary Lawton

Fair Marjorie was sitting in her lower chamber window A combing back her hair, It was there she saw young Willie and his bride A climbing the up-per church stair. She

2. She drew the comb out of her hair
   And flashed it across the floor,
   It was out of the chamber window she jumped,
   She was never seen any more.

3. About the middle part of the night
   When all were fast asleep
   Fair Marjorie appeared in Willie's room
   And stood there at his feet.

4. "Oh how do you like your blanket," she said,
   "And how do you like your sheet,
   And how do you like your new married bride
   Who lies in your arms asleep?"

5. "Very well I like my blanket," he said,
   "Very well I like my sheet,
   But better do I like fair Marjorie
   As she stands there at my feet."

6. She took the comb out of her hair
   And smote him across the breast,
   Saying, "Be prepared and come with me
   To find your final rest."

7. He kissed her once and he kissed her twice
   And he kissed her three times o'er,
   And then he fell there at her feet
   To kiss a woman never more.

"Ellen and her Geese," Cow Head Summerside, 1880,
Dr. Henry N. Payne Community Museum.

9
The Golden Glove

Traditional
Arr. Rosemary Lawton

Tis of a rich merchant in Plymouth town did dwell,
She courted a squire and she loved him full well;
All for to get married it was their intent,
When their friends and relations they all gave consent. The

2. The time being appointed all for the wedding day,
   When the squire went a-choosing his bride-boys to be;
   And when she saw the farmer, "My Charmer," she cried,
   "Oh my joy, oh my joy, oh my charmer," she cried.

3. She turned from the squire and nothing more was said,
   And instead of getting married she went to her bed;
   The thoughts of the farmer fun strong in her mind,
   And a way for her to gain him she quickly did find.

4. Her waistcoat and her britches this fair girl put on,
   And as she went a-hunting with her dog and her gun,
   She hunted all 'round where the farmer did dwell,
   She knew it in her heart that she loved him so well.

5. Often did she fire but nothing did she kill,
   Till at length the young farmer stepped into the field;
   All for to discourse with him it was her intent,
   With her dog and her gun up to meet him she went.

6. Up she did go to her love so bold,
   Saying, "Here is a glove that is flowered with gold."
   Saying, "Here is a glove that I found coming along
   As I was a-hunting with my dog and my gun."

7. Home she did go with her heart full of love,
   She put up a notice that she had lost her glove;
   "And the man that finds it and brings it safe to me,
   The very same night now his bride I will be."

8. The farmer being glad at hearing this great news,
   He went straight unto the lady and begged to be excused.
   "My honourable fair one, I've picked up your glove,
   And I humbly beseech you to grant me your love."

9. "Tis already granted," this fair lady cried,
   "For I love the sweet breath of a farmer," she said,
   "I'll manage my own dairy and I'll milk my own cow,
   And the jolly young farmer will follow the plough."

10. After they were married she told him all the fun
    How she hunted the field with her dog and her gun
    "So now I have got you right safe in my snare,
    Will I ever enjoy you, you pretty little dear."

"Women Making Saltfish," Grand Bank, 1925,
The Rooms Provincial Archives, A-18-173.

10
Gold Watch

Traditional
Arr. Rosemary Lawton

2. I stepped up to her, thinking for to view her;
   I asked this fair maiden where was she a-going,
   Kind kisses I gave her, love to her intending,
   But 'twas all in vain for she was a maid.

3. "I will not, I shall not, I will not go with you;
   I will not go with you for I am afraid.
   My parents will be angry should have a lover;
   My parents will call you a wanton young blade."

4. This made me more anxious and eager than ever,
   For to think I could embrace with a comely fair maid.
   Five guineas she demanded, the money I soon handed,
   When supper being over we both went to bed.

5. As I been a-tired and weary of drinking,
   As I been a-tired and weary of game,
   As I fell a-nodding and she fell a-robbing,
   She picked my pockets of all that I had.

6. I slewed round to kiss her, and I instantly missed her,
   I start for the bolster lied under my head;
   She had robbed me and she had plundered, I roared out like thunder
   But 'twas all in vain for the madam was fled.

7. My gold watch and money, for that I don't value,
   My jewels and riches for that I do mourn,
   I'm afraid that some lady that will be my conductor,
   And I hope that I'll never meet a false girl again.

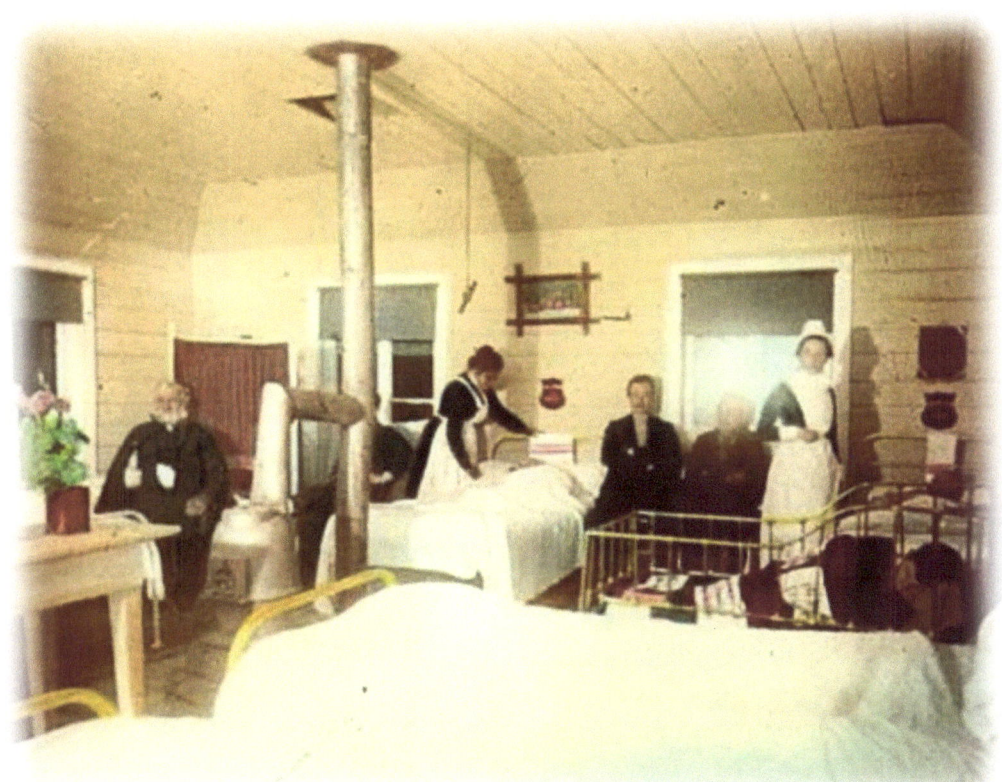

"Battle Harbour Hospital Interior," Battle Harbour, Labrador, 1920,
Maritime History Archive, Memorial University. International Grenfell Association
Lantern Slides Collection

11
Gold Watch and Chain

Traditional
Arr. Rosemary Lawton

2. Early the next morning this girl arose,
   She dressed herself up in sailor's clothes
   To meet her true love on the plain,
   To meet her true love,
   To meet her true love away she goes again.

3. She met her true love all on the strand
   She boldly commanded him all for to stand;
   "Come, deliver up now, young man," she declared,
   "Come, deliver up now,
   Come, deliver it up now and your life I'll spare."

4. He delivered up his gold watch and chain;
   "There is one thing more that I saw you wear,
   It's a diamond ring that shines so fair,
   Come, deliver up now,
   Come, deliver it up now and your life I'll spare.

5. "That diamond ring is a pledge of love.
   Before I'll deliver it my life I'll lose."
   And it became clear to her how true,
   How true was his love,
   An away she run from her own true love.

6. Early the next morning this couple was seen
   A-waking out in some garden green
   With a watch and chain hanging on her clothes
   Which made her blush,
   Which made her blush like a morning rose.

7. What makes you blush at so silly a thing?
   "'Twas I that commanded your diamond ring,
   'Twas I that robbed you on the plain,
   So here's your watch,
   So here's your watch, love, and golden chain."

8. "What made you act such a silly plot?
   If I'd had my pistols 'tis you I'd a-shot,
   Would have left you bleeding all on the plain,
   And then I'd have mourned,
   And then I'd have mourned for the love I'd slain."

12
The Irish Colleen

Traditional
Arr. Rosemary Lawton

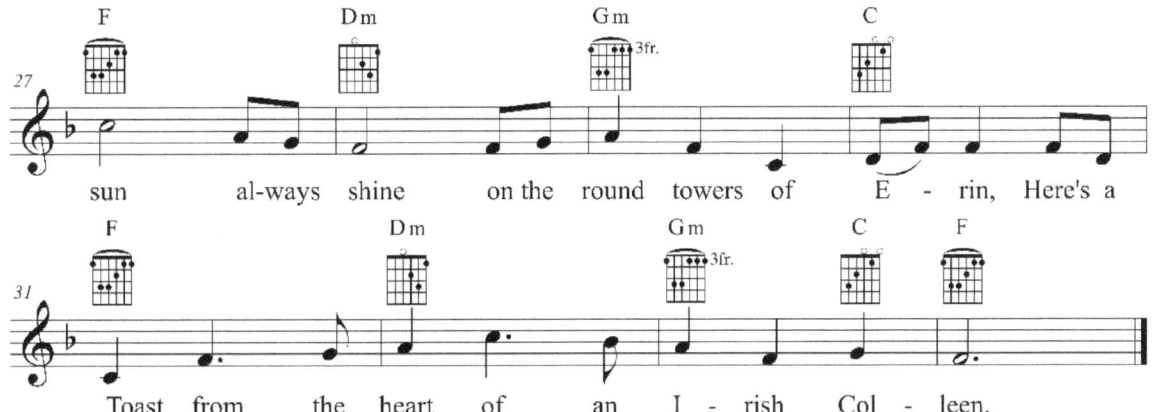

sun al-ways shine on the round towers of E - rin, Here's a Toast from the heart of an I - rish Col - leen.

Reprise:
Then here's to old Ireland, her sons and her daughters,
Here's to old Ireland, the shamrock I mean.
May the sun always shine on the round towers of Erin,
Here's a toast from the heart of an Irish Colleen.

2. The Welsh girl stood up, gave a toast to the leek,
   Saying, "I drink to my emblem each day of the week."
   The Scottish lassie stood up with the pride in her eye,
   Saying, "Here's to the thistle no Scotchman deny."
   The English girl then gave a toast to the rose,
   Saying, "Here's to old England, she can thrash all her foes."
   Buut says I, "I won't willingly cause any pain,
   I ask you to join in my toast once again."

3. We don't hold for the traitors to martyr their cause,
   All we want is justice and good honest laws,
   And the man that's ashamed of the place where he came
   Is no man at all, not worthy of name.
   I own as a flower I'm fond of the rose,
   The fairest of flowers in the garden that grows,
   Though the flowers all resemble there's a vast gulf between,
   The rose, leek, and thistle, and the Irish Colleen.

13
Lady Margaret
(Sweet William's Ghost)

Traditional
Arr. Rosemary Lawton

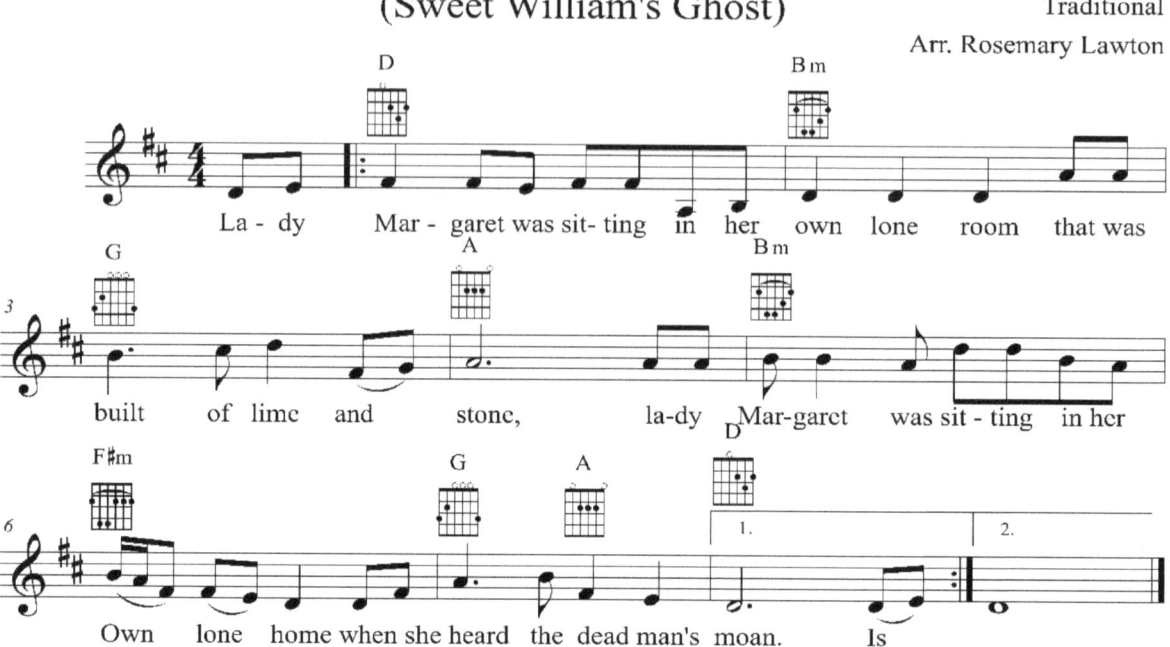

Lady Margaret was sitting in her own lone room that was built of lime and stone, lady Margaret was sitting in her Own lone home when she heard the dead man's moan. Is

2. "Is it my father Thomas?" she said,
   "Or is it my brother John,
   Or my own true love sweet William
   From Scotland home has come?"

3. "'Tis not your father Thomas," he said,
   "'Tis not your brother John,
   But it is your true love William
   From Scotland home has come."

4. "Did you bring me any diamonds or pearls,
   Did you bring to me the ring,
   Did you bring to me any token at all
   That a true love ought to bring?"

5. "I have brought to you no diamonds or pearls,
   I have brought to you no ring,
   But I've brought to you my white winding sheet
   That my body was buried in."

6. "Oh love, where are your red rosy cheeks
   That ofttimes used to bloom?"
   "They are rotten and now are forgotten
   By the love I lost so soon."

7. He took her by the lily-white hand
   And bid her company,
   He took her by the apron band,
   Saying "follow, follow me."

8. She tucked her underskirts one by one
   Just about her knee
   And over the hills on a cold winter's night
   In a dead man's company.

9. They walked and they talked alone together
   Till the cocks began to crow.
   "It's time for the dead and the living to part,
   Lady Margaret I must go."

10. "Is there any room at your head?" she said,
    Is there any room at your feet?
    Is there any room about you at all
    Where I may lie down and sleep?"

11. "My father is at my head," he said,
    "And my mother is at my feet,
    And there's three Hell Hounds lie about my side
    Where my poor soul should sleep."

12. "One is for my drunkenness,
    Another is for my pride,
    And the other is for promising a fair pretty maid
    That should be my bride."

13. She took a cross all from her bosom,
    And she smoted him on the breast
    Saying, "Here's a token for you sweet William,
    God grant you a happy night's rest."

14. "I am thankful to you Lady Margaret," he said,
    "I am thankful unto you,
    If the dead are bound to pray for the living
    Then I shall pray for you.

15. "Good night, good night Lady Margaret," he said.
    "Good night, good night," said she,
    "I hope the very next time we do meet
    In heaven we both shall be."

14
The Lovely Lowland Maid

Traditional
Arr. Rosemary Lawton

2. "Good morning to you Mary Ann, I'm glad I met with you,
   Have you forgot your old true love or changed the old for new?
   What is your inclination? Come tell to me I pray."
   "begone from me," cried Mary Ann, that lovely lowland maid.

3. As Mary Ann one evening sat in her cottage door
   She frowned on her sailor because he looked so poor.
   "Oh what is your intention? Come all to me I pray."
   "I pray begone," cried Mary Ann that lovely lowland maid.

4. At those feeling words the lady spoke the sailor cried, "Behold!"
   When from his pocket hauled out a purse of gold.
   "Excuse me now," cried Mary Ann, "Excuse me what I said,
   You're welcome to my cottage and the lovely lowland maid."

5. "Begone deceitful Mary Ann, your way it is well paid,
   Sure I can stay till morning in some lonely barn or shed,
   Sure I can stay till morning in some lonely barn or shed."
   And he wandered to the stable from that lovely lowland maid.

6. 'Twas at the hour of twelve o'clock false Mary Ann did say
   Unto another suitor, "We will have him betrayed."
   And when they reached the stable where the sailor lay,
   "Oh slay him in his slumber!" Cried the lovely lowland maid.

7. They plunged their fatal daggers within the sailor's breast,
   They robbed him of his glittering gold and laid him there to rest.
   A keeper he being watching al from the wood he strayed,
   He swore against that villain and the lovely lowland maid.

8. The villain he was taken, those words I heard him say:
   "I would not have killed the sailor, only for being persuade."
   They looked at each other upon their trial day.
   This villain was condemned to die with the lovely lowland maid.

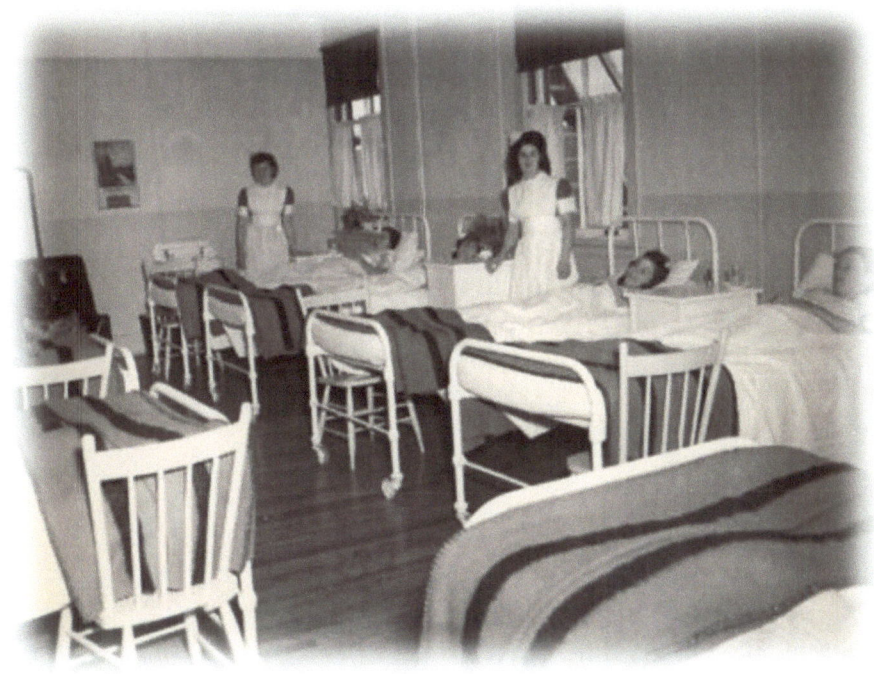

"Bonavista Cottage Hospital," Bonavista, Newfoundland, 1947,
Maritime History Archive, Memorial University. PF-318.290. Forbes Family Fonds.

15
Maiden Who Dwelt by the Shore
(Maid on the Shore)

Traditional
Arr. Rosemary Lawton

'Twas of a young maiden who lived all a-lone, She lived all a-lone on the shore, O, there was no-thing she could find but to com-fort her mind but to roam all a-lone on the shore, shore, shore, But to roam all a-lone on the shore. 'Twas

2. 'Twas of a young captain who sailed the salt sea,
   Let the wind blow high or blow low, O,
   "I will die, I will die," the young captain did cry,
   If I can't get that maid on the shore, shore, shore,
   If I can't get that maid on the shore."

3. "I have lots of silver, I have lots of gold,
   I have lots of costly wear, O;
   I'll divide, I'll divide with my jolly ship's crew,
   If they'll row me that maid from the shore, shore, shore,
   If they'll row me that maid fro the shore."

4. After much persuasion they got her on board,
   Let the winds blow high or low, O,
   They placed her away in his cabin below;
   "Here's adieu to all sorrows and care, care, care,
   Here's adieu to all sorrows and care."

5. They placed her away in his cabin below
   Let the winds blow high or blow low, O,
   She's so pretty and sweet, she's so neat and complete,
   She sang captain and sailors to sleep, sleep, sleep,
   She sang captain and sailors to sleep.

6. She robbed him of silver, she robbed him of gold,
   She robbed him of costly wear, O,
   She took his broad sword instead of an oar,
   And she paddled her way to the shore, shore, shore,
   And she paddled her way to the sore.

7. "My men must be crazy, my men must be mad,
   My men must been deep in despair, O,
   For to let her away with her beauty so gay,
   And paddle her way to the shore, shore, shore,
   And paddle her way to the shore."

8. "Your men was not crazy, your men was not mad,
   Your men was not deep in despair, O,
   I deluded your sailors as well as yourself;
   I'm a maiden again on the shore, shore, shore,
   I'm a maiden again on the shore."

"Nurse Myra Grimsley Bennett," 1915,
Nurse Myra Bennett Foundation.

16
The Old Woman

Traditional
Arr. Rosemary Lawton

2. Jack came in all in the dark,
   Looking for his dear sweetheart.
   He hit his toe into the chair
   And smashed up all the crock'ry ware.

Reprise:
To me wee wack fal liddle I day, O,
To me wee wack fal liddle I day, O.

3. She came all in a fright
   Calling for her candle light,
   She said "Young man what brought you here,
   Smashing up my crock'ry ware?"

4. He says, "Old woman, don't be so cross;
   I lost my way into a loss."
   He says, "Old woman don't be cross;
   I lost my way into a loss."

5. Here's four pounds for your broken chair,
   And ten pounds ten for your crock'ry ware.
   Here's ten pounds ten for your broken chair,
   And ten pounds ten for your crock'ry ware.

6. Come all young men who have sweethearts,
   Never go courting in the dark,
   For if you do you'll find it dear
   A trippin' round in the crock'ry wear.

"Wash day on the Coast," Labrador, between 1929 and 1934,
Rooms Provincial Archives, VA 114-48,
International Grenfell Association photograph collection.

17
The Outlandish Knight
(Lady Isobel and the Elf Knight)

Traditional
Arr. Rosemary Lawton

Give me some of your da - da's gold and some of your ma - ma's fee, and the ve - ry best nag in your fa - ther's barn - where there lies thir - ty and three

2. He rode till he came to a river-side
   Alight, alight, says he;
   Six fair maids I have drowned here
   And you the seventh shall be

3. Six fair pretty maids you have drowned here
   And why do you do so by me?
   You promised that you'd marry me
   And both would married be

4. Take off your rich, your costly robe
   And lay it down by me,
   For it is too rich and too costly
   To rot in the salty sea.

5. turn, O turn, young Willie, she says
   O turn your back to me
   Pretty Polly she took him into her arms
   And threw him into the sea

6. Lie there, lie there, false Willie, she says,
   Lie there instead of me,
   You thought to strip me as I was born,
   Not one lack did I take from thee.

7. And then she mounted her meelyer bright
   And faced the green apple tree.
   She rode along, along and along
   This long fine summer's day.

"Newfoundland Suffragists," ca. 1920s Courtesy of Gertrude Crosbie and Archives and Special Collections (Collection 158), Queen Elizabeth II Library, Memorial University.

18
The Press Gang

Traditional
Arr. Rosemary Lawton

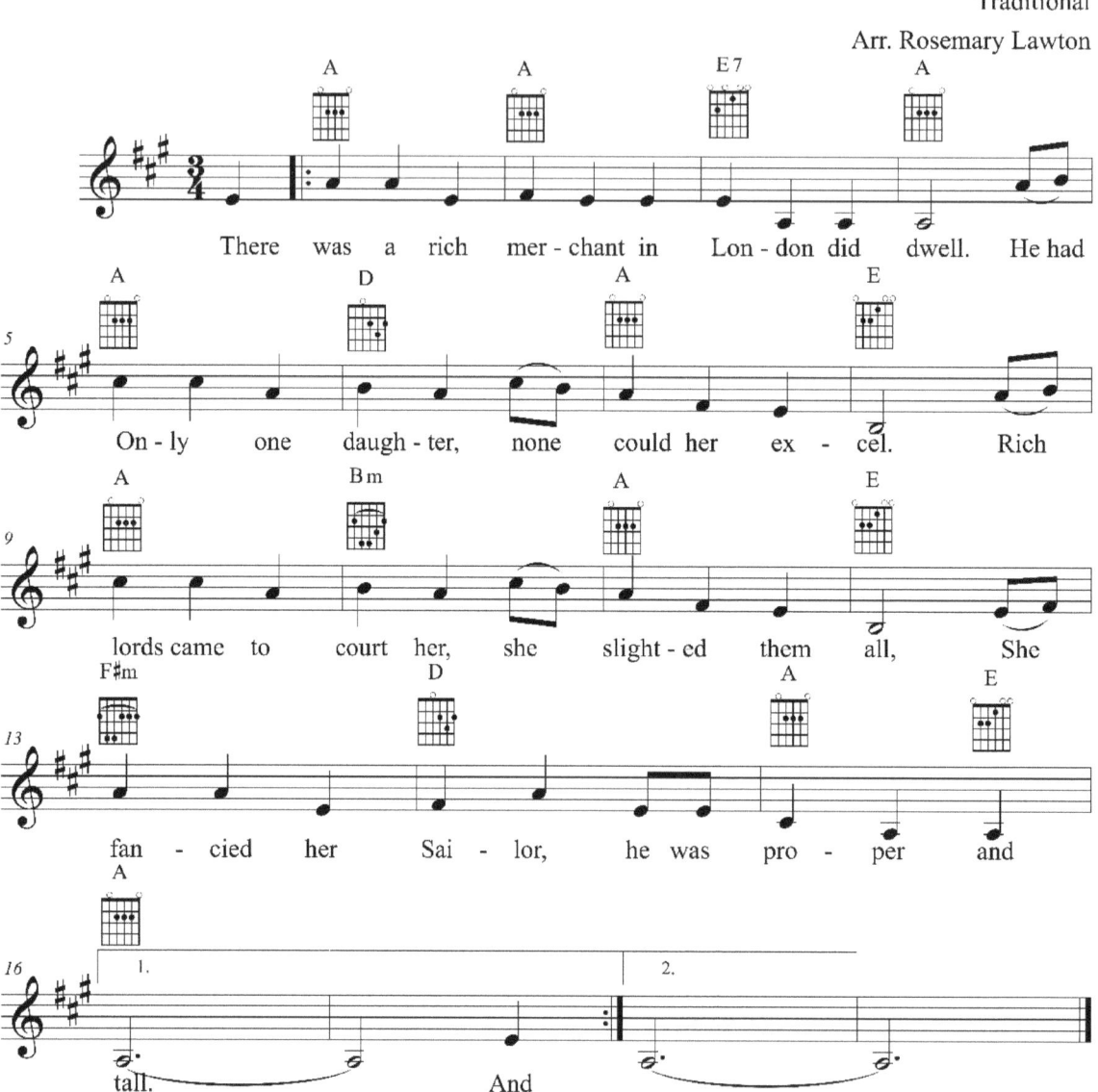

2. And when her old father came this for to hear,
   'Twas on her love William his vengeance did swear:
   You can get better matches your arms to embrace
   Than to marry a sailor your friends to disgrace.

3. pardon me, father, O pardon me, sir,
   There is none in this world but a sailor for me;
   A sailor's my true love and I'll be his bride,
   And if I don't gain him my life I'd destroy.

4. What, what, cried her father, what, what, he did say,
   You must court him in private and speak not of me,
   And when all things is ready I'll surely agree,
   And when all things is ready I'll surely agree.

5. As the lady and sailor walked by the sea shore,
   The press gang surrounded him and half a score more.
   They pressed my own true love and they tore him from me,
   Instead of great mirth 'twas a sorrowful day.

6. This lady she dressed herself up in men's clothes,
   Straightaway to the captain she immediately goes.
   She signed as a sailor and it fell to her lot
   To lie with her true love, but he knew her not.

7. As the lady and the sailor was ploughing the deep,
   Said the lady to the sailor: you sigh in your sleep.
   I once had a true love, the sailor did say,
   'Twas by her cruel father I was sent away.

8. I am an astrologer brought up by pen,
   Astrologer's books I do read now and then.
   If you tell me your name and I'll cast out your lot
   And see if you'll gain that fair lady or not.

9. He told her his name and the hour of his birth.
   She says: you were born for right joy and for mirth;
   You shall gain this fair one in spite of them all,
   So here is your Ellen just now at your call.

10. This couple got married before the ship's crew;
    Which proves this fair damsel to be constant and true;
    And they're now sailing over to old England's fair shore
    Here's a fig for her father she'll never see more.

19
The Pride of the Shamrock Shore

Traditional
Arr. Rosemary Lawton

2. I boldly stepped up to her, and this to her I then did say:
   "I think I'm quite forgotten since I have been so long away,
   But if you will prove constant and try to change your love once more,
   I vow I'd ne'er be parted from Mary the pride of the Shamrock Shore."

3. "Young man oh stop your fretting, for really I don't know what you mean,
   The squire is my true love and I am his precious queen;
   But once I had a sweetheart and now, alas, he is no more,
   Young man do not insult us," Said Mary the pride of the Shamrock Shore.

4. The squire raged with anger saying, "I have powder if skill you'll try,
   A brace of loaded pistols I carry on the lonesome way,
   And if you say you love her it's instantly you are no more,
   So let us fight for true love and Mary the pride of the Shamrock Shore."

5. Twas then the battle did commence and tears from Mary's eyes did flow.
   Young Henry being so valiant the squire he fell with a deadly blow.
   'Twas with the squire's weapon young Mary fired undauntedly;
   She fired and killed her true love, so mortally she gave her wound.

6. 'Twas by one private token that instantly her love she knew,
   she kissed his lips quite cold and o'r the plain distracted flew.
   And there she lies in dark dungeon, Mary lies forever more,
   With prison walls around her lies Mary the pride of the Shamrock Shore.

"Hannah Michlin holding rifle, standing with her husband," Rigolet, Labrador, 1893,
The Rooms Provincial Archives, VA 152-130,
MG 152 Eliot Curwen Fonds photograph collection.

20
The Rose of Britain's Isle

Traditional
Arr. Rosemary Lawton

2. She was a merchant's daughter,
   Her father's only joy.
   Until she fell in love with
   Her father's prentice boy.
   His cheeks were like the roses
   And his face appears to smile.
   By all above he swore he'd love
   The Rose of Britain's Isle.

3. When her old aged father heart
   That he was courting her,
   He wrung his hands and tore his hair,
   Most bitterly did swear,
   Saying: Before you'll bring disgrace on me
   I'll send you many a mile
   With great disdain across the main
   From the Rose of Britain's Isle.

4. Young Edwin went on board the ship
   For to cross over the main,
   While Jane alone in anguish moaned,
   Her bosom heaved with pain.
   She dressed herself in mans attire
   And after a little while
   On board the ship with young Edwin went
   The Rose of Britain's Isle.

5. When they were crossing the coasts of Spain
   The enemy gave alarm.
   'Twas by a ball young Jane did fall
   And wounded her right arm.
   The sailors ran to lend a hand
   While Jane on them did smile.
   The sailors swore by all on board
   'Twas the Rose of Britain's Isle.

6. Young Edwin he being thunderstruck,
   His heart was filled with pain.
   As soon as Jane recovered
   They sailed across the main;
   As soon as Jane recovered
   And after a little while
   Back home again with Edwin gay,
   The Rose of Britain's Isle.

7. Her father he being dead and gone,
   Now joys are to relate,
   He willed a handsome fortune
   Likewise a large estate.
   He willed a handsome fortune
   And after a little while,
   Young Edwin he made Jane his bride
   The Rose of Britain's Isle.

21
Rosy Banks of Green

Traditional
Arr. Rosemary Lawton

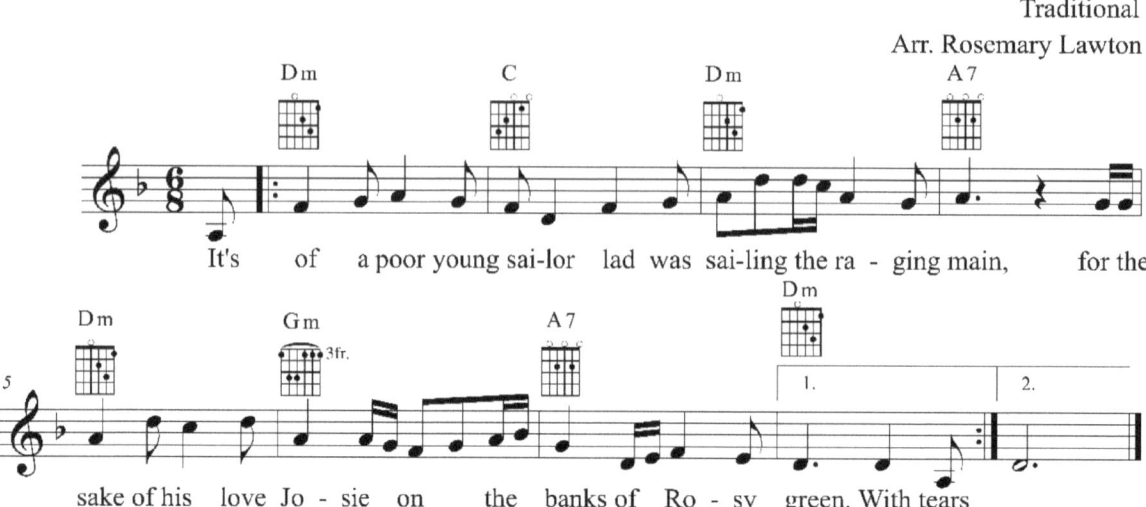

It's of a poor young sai-lor lad was sai-ling the ra-ging main, for the sake of his love Jo-sie on the banks of Ro-sy green. With tears

2. With tears and fond embraces his only Josephine,
   "We never shall be parted on the rosy banks of green."
   Her father overheard them and his anger could not stand;
   He jumped in front of them a loaded gun in his right hand.

3. He aimed that deadly weapon and that fateful trigger drew,
   And Josephine like lightening to her lover's arms she flew;
   The bullet sped its course and so truly was his aim,
   And those two fell a victim on the rosy banks of green.

4. As Josephine lay dying, these words I heard her say,
   "I'm glad my poor old mother never lived to see this day,
   O Charlie, my dear Charlie, you will never see again,
   Your aged parents you will never see again no more.

5. "But may you live in glory with your only Josephine,
   And never shall be parted on the rosy banks of green."
   Beneath the marble tombstone it is down by a purling stream
   Sleeps these two constant lovers on the rosy banks of green.

"Two Girls Roll Barrels Down the Warf," Hopedale, 1914,
The Rooms Provincial Archives, VA 72-63.5, John B. Bisbee, John Bancroft Bisbee Fonds.

22
The Soldier Maid

Traditional
Arr. Rosemary Lawton

2. With my feather in my hat I will have you all to see,
   My officer he taught me a stately man to be,
   The soldiers all admired me, my fingers were so small,
   And they learned me to beat upon the drum the best of all.

3. Oh when I went to my quarters the night time for the spend,
   I was not ashamed for to lie among the men,
   And hauling off my small clothes to myself I ofttimes smiled,
   A-lying with the soldiers a maid all the while.

4. Oh many were the battles that I fought upon the field,
   And many a brave fellow was forced from me to yield.
   I was guarded by my general for fear I would be slain,
   And for cruelty they sent me back to old England again.

5. Then they sent me over to London to take charge of the tower,
   I never was discovered until that day and hour,
   When a lady fell in love with me I told her I was a maid,
   And straight unto my regiment my secrets were betrayed.

6. Then up the steps the officer, he made no more to-do,
   He asked to me the question, I answered him quite true.
   He laughed at the joke and he smiled and he said:
   "It's a pity we should lose such a drummer as a maid."

7. Here's a health to the Duke, here's a health, sir, unto you,
   Here's a health to every British man who keeps his courage true.
   And if our King does want more men those Frenchmen to be slain,
   I will boldly stand with sword in hand and fight for him again.

"Making Hay," 1940,
Trinity Historical Society

23
Willy Taylor

Traditional
Arr. Rosemary Lawton

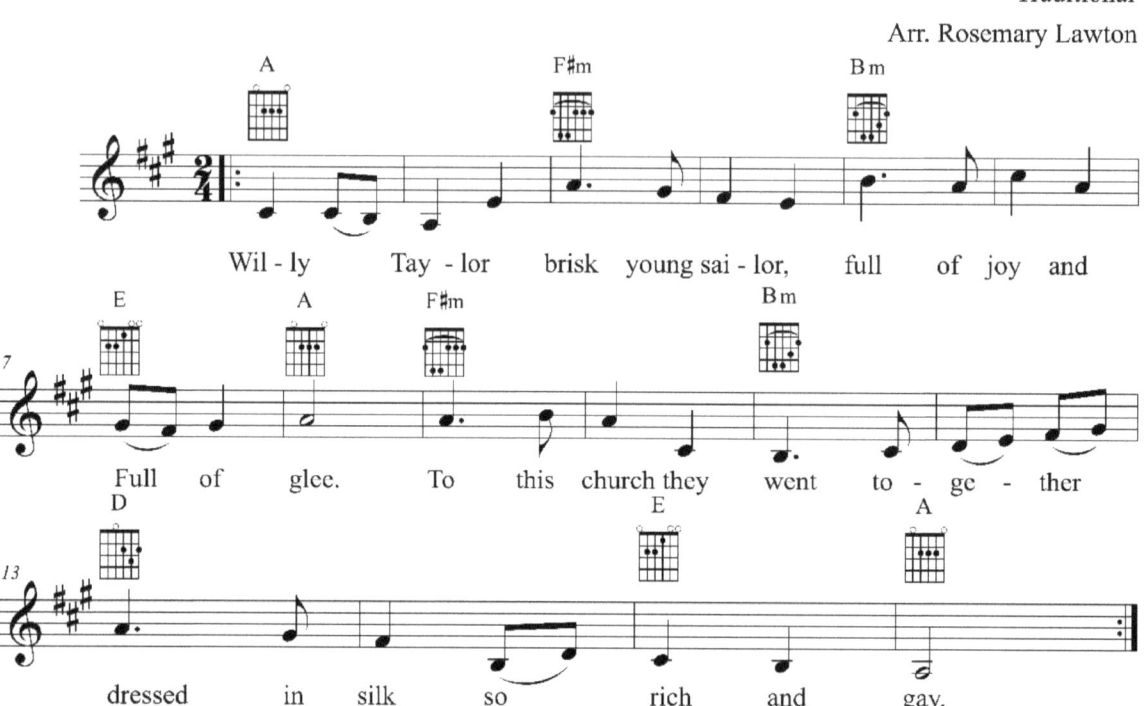

Wil - ly Tay - lor brisk young sai - lor, full of joy and Full of glee. To this church they went to - ge - ther dressed in silk so rich and gay.

2. Bells were ringing, children singing,
   At the church they went that day;
   In the church went twenty sailors,
   Pressed young Willie off to sea.

3. Soon the fair one followed after,
   Went in name of Richard Car;
   Then her hands and lily fingers
   Soon embraced the pitch and tar.

4. Now she's on the ocean sailing,
   Two broad swords in all her hand.
   Then her vest coat it blew open
   And they spied their lily breast.

5. When the Captain came to hear it,
   Asked what wonders brought her here.
   "I'm in search for my true lover,
   Whom you've pressed from me so dear."

6. "If you're searching for your true love,
   Pray tell what his name might be?"
   "He is named young Willie Taylor,
   Seven years he has gone from me."

7. "You rise early the next morning,
   Just before the break of day,
   There you'll spy young Willie Taylor,
   Walking with some lady gay."

8. She rose early the next morning,
   Just before the break of day;
   There she spied young Willie Taylor,
   Walking with some lady gay.

9. Then she called for two bright pistols;
   They were brought at her command,
   Up and shot young Willy Taylor,
   Standing by his bride's right hand.

10. When the Captain came to hear it,
    Asked what wonders she had done,
    Then he made her first lieutenant,
    Board a ship nine hundred tons.

11. Now she's on the ocean sailing;
    Two broad swords all in her hand;
    Every time that ship made motion,
    They'd all tremble at her command.

"Inuit woman with children," 1920, Maritime History Archive, Memorial University, PF-323.057, International Grenfel Association

REFERENCES

Greenleaf, Elizabeth B., and Mansfield, Grace Y., editor. *Ballads and Sea Songs of Newfoundland.* 2nd ed., Memorial U of Newfoundland, 1968.

Karpeles, Maud, editor. *Folk Songs from Newfoundland.* Faber and Faber Limited, 1971.

Leach, MacEdward, editor. *Folk Ballads and Songs of the Lower Labrador Coast.* Queen's Printer/National Museum of Canada, 1965.

Peacock, Kenneth, editor. *Songs of the Newfoundland Outports.* Vol. 2, Queen's Printer/National Museum of Canada, 1965.

OTHER RESOURCES

Lehr, Genevieve, editor. *Come and I will Sing You: A Newfoundland songbook.* U of Toronto Press, 1985.

ABOUT THE AUTHOR

Rosemary Lawton, 2019 ECMA Roots/Traditional nominee, 2018 MusicNL Celtic/Traditional and Female Artist of the Year nominee, is an up-and-coming force within the Newfoundland music scene.

Rosemary is a multi-award-nominated Newfoundland traditional artist, with a Bachelor of Music with a focus in violin, and a Bachelor of Music Education from Memorial University of Newfoundland. She is a passionate advocate of women's issues and champions the advancement of women in the music industry through her work.

Rosemary is helping to preserve Newfoundland and Labrador's rich tradition by collecting, recording, and performing traditional music throughout the province.

www.ingramcontent.com/pod-product-compliance
Lightning Source LLC
Chambersburg PA
CBHW042010150426
43195CB00002B/75